PEDACITOS: LITTLE PIECES

ISBN-13 (print): 979-8-9877417-4-0
ISBN (ebook): 979-8-9877417-2-6

Library of Congress Control Number: 2025904801


All inquiries and requests should be addressed to the author: www.cristalgonzalezavila.com.

Cover art and illustrations by: Ariel Mar
Edited by: Elizabeth Cisneros
Foreword by: Luis Valdez


Set in Raleway


First US Edition 2025
San Juan Bautista, California

Published by Ocote Libre Press
www.ocotelibrepress.com

little pieces

Pedacitos

By: Cristal González Ávila

OCOTE LIBRE PRESS

San Juan Bautista, California

Written By: Cristal González Ávila
Illustrated by: Ariel Mar
Edited by: Elizabeth Cisneros

para mi Madre

**Table of Contents**

# FOREWORD by Luis Valdez

Aquí se oye la voz más clara de Cristal González Ávila. It is a voice as crystal clear as a mountain stream, a voice emanating from the transparent heart of a Chicana . . . poet, playwright, actor, teacher, wife and young mother of two beautiful daughters.

This is her story, the "pedacitos" of her life's journey. From childhood to puberty and beyond, from her first memories of a happy home to the shattering of her childhood's innocence, from a daughter's love for her mother's resilience in the face of betrayal by body and soul, to her painful relationship with her father.

It is written in a style bilingual readers will appreciate and understand, but that is part of the magic of these "little pieces" of her life. Her voice resonates with authenticity and humility, touching the heart as much as the mind in her carefully crafted code-switching narrative. Spanish and

English phrases freely dance around each other in all her accounts, capturing the tones required by her emotional honesty. We not only hear her story, we are able to feel it. At least those who can identify with it can, having lived life in two languages.

On a simply universal level, Cristal's narrative touches on her conscious evolution from a child to a teenager to a woman, as she discovers and explores her natural magnetism toward the performing arts. She senses and decides early on that she wants to be "an actor." Getting there requires overcoming all the obstacles in her way – including poverty, racism, sexism, and secret abuse. Gaining confidence as she goes – she finally discovers the liberating power of her storytelling. And that brings us back to the simply complex beauty of this narrative. Cristal is able to reveal the shape of her early life by arranging these critical "pedacitos" in such a way that they suggest the whole.

I have heard Cristal's voice before as a playwright

and core member of El Teatro Campesino. Her plays and monologues speak in the same tone and with the same brilliant clarity as these short vignettes.

It is thus my privilege to introduce a toda nuestra gente the unique voice of this emerging remarkable writer, Cristal González Ávila.

little pieces

Pedacitos

By: Cristal González Ávila

## 22 Melrose

Mi casa. Azul y blanca, con escalones color rojo ladrillo. Una chimenea grande que parecía tocar las estrellas. A two-story house with three large windows overseeing el zacate verde que Papá tanto cuidaba. Home, with a spacious backyard where we lost track of time playing basketball, riding bikes, celebrating life. Donde quebrábamos piñatas y soplábamos deseos cada cumpleaños, where our dog Jasmine is buried beneath a large oak tree. Nuestra casita, donde corríamos de cualquier lugar al escuchar la troquita de Papá llegar.

As we drove away, I heard the "Feliz Cumpleaños" and "Merry Christmas," the voice of our nana Rebecca who we called Jafar yelling "¡¡¡niñas!!!". El Mariachi cantando "Mi linda esposa" en el patio de atrás. Todo, todo pasó por mi mente por un largo instante, como si un pedacito de mí se estuviera muriendo lentamente.

Nuestra casita. White with navy blue trimmings, dark green trees outlining the parameters of our home. A brick-red colored four-step staircase leading to the front door as the signature touch of our Gonzalez home. 22 Melrose where it all began and vanished como una nube pasajera. Donde todo comenzó y terminó. Una casa llena de sueños y sueños rotos. En el invierno del '95 mi Papá se fue. Meses después perdimos la casa, y así fue como nos perdimos todas. We all witnessed parts of each other die in slow motion, unable to react in real time. We stood and watched our home walls cave in on themselves, dejando solo pedazos de lo que un día fue. There was no time to mourn. Todas levantamos la cabeza sin dirección segura pusimos un paso tras otro and we left.

We closed the door to 22 Melrose and drove away from our casa, just like Papá, only without Papá.

# La mujer en mi vida

Mi Madre is a beautiful spirit with an exaggerated laugh. During her teen years, she wanted nothing more than to be a nun. She admired their grace but feared my grandparents' judgment y se quedó con sus deseos silenciosamente. Mamá was brought up Catholic, and her faith has been her strength. La Virgen de Guadalupe was her loyal confidant and the rosary her weapon in life.

Mamá enjoyed being in the company of strangers. We would pick up "gente que acababa de llegar" too often. It usually happened when we would go to La Esperanza Meat Market right after paying el mandado. We headed home with bags of groceries and a handful of compañeros. There was always an extra taco de frijol to offer our fellow paisanos.

"¡Venganse! Vamos a la casa para que coman un taco." Mamá would tell them. They followed us into the car without saying a  word, just a humble nod.

Sometimes, there were as many as seven of us at once, including Mamá y yo, rumbo al apartamento. The beat-up blue 90's Taurus Ford that looked more like a low-rider carrying too much weight. The smell of sweat and dirt fogging up the windows, empty stomachs humming, timid compañeros singing along to the melancholy voice of Ana Gabriel on the radio and sighing entre canciones. And if that wasn't enough to get some miradas our way, the word BITCH that had been carved into the hood of the car by some cholas from the Meadow View apartments we lived at before, gave our carrazo the final touch.

Money was scarce so we concealed the BITCH carving with a glossy blue nail polish, making matters worse. Despacio pero bien proud, the nail polished BITCH Ford low-rider drove down Main Street and turned right onto Rodriguez Street, three blocks away from La Esperanza.

I questioned if the recién llegados would go to La Esperanza, which means "hope" in English, porque they were hopeful life would take a different route en los Estados Unidos. Mamá slowly got out of the car and made her way to the apartment with her walker sustaining her desire to help others. Meanwhile I would run to our apartment a calentar frijoles and tortillas de maíz, cut some queso fresco en pedazos largos and smelled the chile colorado to make sure it was still good. Before we knew it, lunch was ready.

In essence, that was Mamá, always taking the opportunity to help others. Dando lo poco que teníamos porque donde come uno, pueden comer cinco.

Mi Madre, a reflection of strength, compasión y mucho amor. A mujer warrior wounded, fighting the ache courageously.

I sit here and wonder: when did she surrender her fight, and why didn't I see it?

# Dino & la bailarina mexicana

Johnny was Denise's younger cousin and Denise was my older sister Diana's best friend since high school, maybe even middle school. Johnny was the first boy I kissed over a game of truth or dare in the Meadow View apartment's pool. We were little mocosos, a peck but nevertheless it was a beso. Johnny defended me at school from Juan Carlos who we called Casper because of his pale skin. Unlike Casper the friendly ghost, Juan Carlos was sangrón, de carácter pesado. He always wanted to get close to me and kiss me, finally one day I slapped him.

Johnny estaba allí, he smiled after la cachetada que le di a Casper y salimos corriendo al recreo.

Johnny was the first person I trusted outside my home. The only friend in my childhood to ask me, "¿Qué tiene tu Mamá? What happened to your Mom?" We had been friends since I could remember, it's like he had always been there. Our tender hearts communicated in a mysterious unspoken way. Sin palabras sabíamos cuando ocupabamos un abrazo, espacio and even a good laugh. He was my favorite person to be next to during school events and even more so during the Halloween parade. Sin decir nada we would hold hands.

This year I would be a ballerina for Halloween—a pink Ballerina with too much nalga for a second grader. My sister Diana bought me a costume at a second-hand shop en Santa Cruz. I remember it was late when she got home. The telenovela *Agujetas de color de rosa* was on, and I was fighting sleep to finish the episode. She walked in carrying several plastic bags, she gathered all my sisters and told us all what we were going to be for Halloween.

"Cristal, you're the ballerina."

"Yes!!" I began undressing but Mamá stopped me and sent me to bed. I kissed my sisters goodnight, got Mamá's blessing, "en el nombre del Padre, del Hijo, y del Espíritu Santo, Amén," picked-up my amazing costume, stuffed it in my backpack and called it a night.

At school, the Halloween parade was like a desfile of quién tiene más dinero, pero no contaban con la imaginación de mi familia. Mi Mamá and Diana eran las reinas of doing more with less. All the kids were encouraged to bring their costumes and change in class for the midday parade. There were beautiful bejeweled Disney princesses, expensive pirates and scary Chucky costumes with blood stains. Mine was elegant, classy, sencillo pero bonito; at least I thought. I was certain I would feel pretty and maybe have a chance of winning the Unique Costume prize this year. Silly me!

Johnny wore the same costume as last year, a cute green dinosaur. I smiled as he made his way back to his seat. He shrugged, not thrilled about being the dino again, but he made the best out of it. I noticed he had gotten taller, este año se estiró and I could see his ankles peeking out of his jumpsuit.

It was my turn to change, I couldn't wait! All the little girls were taken behind a dressing room, which was really a bunch of tables and a couple of ropes with sábanas. The teacher's aide helped us dress into our

costumes. That morning, I didn't pay much attention to the chonis I was wearing. After all, I was only seven. Pero Monica, a classmate with a funny lisp who took joy in embarrassing others, made it public.

"Ewww, you have Barney underwear!"

As she pointed my way and giggled, I slowly looked down to confirm she was right. I was wearing old purple Barney chonis. I had an instant stomach ache and couldn't help but feel the blood rushing to my face. Suddenly I started sweating. I continued dressing and ignored her comments and all the other miradas that immediately came my way. The girls kept riéndose and I couldn't stop trembling. So there I was, behind some makeshift dressing room, trying to put my ballerina costume on. I hadn't tried it on at home the night before because it was past my bedtime. I guess my sister figured it would fit, but it didn't! Well, at least not in my butt. The leotard didn't cover my underwear, and my pink tights didn't hide the big purple Barney chonis.

Monica continued, "You can't be a ballerina, you're

Mexican." Then, she laughed like one of those hyenas from the *Lion King* movie.

I tried really hard not to cry. Y de repente, I didn't feel so pretty anymore; I felt more like a piñata that everyone was ready to take a swing at. Todas listas para quebrarme.

I attempted to hide my undies under my leotard, stretching the leotard to the sides hoping this would give me some coverage. I pulled down the tutu to cover my bottom but it didn't do anything. Barney wouldn't go away! I walked out of the dressing room sintiéndome más fea que cuando entré. I turned to my friend Johnny and he smiled extra big, he even added two thumbs-up.

The parade was a blur but I do remember he held my hand.

# Starlight, Star-Bright

**Diana.** DEE. Diana Maribel although she never liked her middle name, **Di-ah-na.**

Mi hermana mayor, la jefa, chingona, luchadora, fashionista y bien criticona. Always figuring out how to keep the refrigerator full, the food stamps mailed our way, finding health care for Mamá, paying bills on top of bills, keeping it all inside – possibly blowing up but out of sight. Her pride kept her from crumbling like a mazapán, hiding behind her colgate smile.

At seventeen, mi hermanita was forced to become the best version of herself, she had to be the best - for all of us. Overnight, pushing her dreams to the side and taking up all the deserted responsibilities Dad left behind.

In 1995 Diana became the host of the "Christmas Talent Show," a tradition that saved Navidad gatherings for years to come. The crowd went wild, song after song; we must have performed the entire "Selena Greatest Hits" collection that Christmas Eve. I sang, danced, channeled Selena to perfection, or so I was told. It was somewhere between the washing machine spins and hand gestures, while *Como la Flor* blasted in the background, I felt free, like I levitated. Libre, como el viento en el invierno.

After that Christmas performance, I made my public debut at the Starlight Elementary Talent Show. I performed Selena's "I Will Survive (Funky Town)!" It had a great beat and in many ways I was still very much "surviving." I was new to Starlight, we moved from 22 Melrose to Meadow View Apartments from H.A. Hyde to Starlight Elementary School. I was terrified; making friends wasn't something I was looking forward to. I missed holding Johnny's hand.

It was a month into the school year when Randy came into the class to make an announcement.

Randy had really big glasses with thick lenses as if

he were always looking through a microscope. Era calvo, pale shiny-glossy skin, and chaparro. Not too much of a talker, in the month that I had been there, I hadn't heard Randy speak more than two words at a time. During recess he would yell: "Be careful! I'm watching!" or "line-up!" and pretty much the same thing after school as we waited for the giant twinkie buses to arrive.

"We'll be having tryouts for Starlights' talent show on Friday and the Talent Show will be the following Friday," Randy said, in a monotone kind of way.

Not too many of my classmates looked excited but I was ready to jump off my seat and begin showing him my moves. I inhaled, contained my excitement and went about my day. Pero the truth was I couldn't wait to go home and tell my sister Diana all about it.

As soon as she arrived, I exploded with joy.

"Randy! The bald yard duty guy told the class today that there's going to be tryouts for the school talent show. What do you think? Maybe Selena?"

Without saying a word, Diana and I drove down Main Street to the Discount Mall looking for the best Selena outfit. We walked and walked, passing by exaggerated, ugly Quinceañera dresses with big football shoulders, chamarras de fake cuero and underwear for men with slim colorful elephant noses in the front. Yuck! ¡Qué asco! There was nothing Selena-ish about this place.

At The Discount Mall, you can get anything from a tongue piercing to recuerdos for the bautismo. We walked in circles until we found it! It was there, waiting for me! A two-piece light purple top and bell-bottoms, like Selena's, well kinda, minus the glittery flair. Diana bought it without hesitation, it was perfect. It was a little tight on my baby belly but I didn't care I was Selena with a panza.

Next day I tried-out and got in.

The following Friday came sooner than I expected, but I was prepared; I practiced everyday after school.

The song began to play, my heart jumping out of my already tight top. I couldn't stop smiling. I started off with three fabulous turns, and the rest was history.

The crowd cheered and I kept moving to precision leaving no doubt of my artistry.

The world made sense when I stood on a stage; everything else went away. That world saved me. There, I was no longer surviving – I was living, breathing. My sister Diana saved me, and I don't think she knows that.

# Eva

I met Eva in 4th grade. This was the year I had been placed in an English-only class. Before that, I comfortably danced between español and English. Now I wasn't allowed to speak Spanish in class. How do you keep a pajarito from flying?

Eva (E- vah) is pronounced in English, never in Spanish, she tells everyone she meets. She was my daily nightmare. I had to sit next to her every single day. The 4th grade teacher thought she was doing us a favor by sitting students that looked alike next to each other. We had similar features: heavy black hair, canela-colored skin, and we were both of Mexican descent. Pero mi maestra no sabía que yo me iba a un hogar muy distinto, un hogar que Eva ni siquiera podía imaginar. Her world and mine eran muy diferentes. I had more in common with la güerita Hannah. Hannah and her mom lived in the same apartment complex que yo.

Eva was lean, tall for a fourth grader, and according to her, they had a huge home. Her father drove her to school in his Lexus, and practiced basketball with her after school. Her mom was bilingual and had an office job. Eva was one of the few kids who took lunch to school, todos los pinches días. Mom made her delicious sandwiches like the ones in the stupid Oscar Mayer's commercials, and she ate them like the kids en esos comerciales. Her uniform was always pressed to impress and her black doll shoes brillosos con los cute calcetines that have a wavy preppy trim. Any opportunity she had she spoke about her perfect family.

"We shop at Nob Hill, not those Mexican stores."

You have to have money to shop at Nob Hill Foods, not food stamps. Nob Hill was the Beverly Hills of Watson. The further away you lived from it the less well off your familia was. I lived on the other side of town, a mile away from the Pajaro bridge, in Section 8 housing. Mi familia only drove by Nob Hill, on our way to catch the HWY 1 towards Santa Cruz.

In the newspaper ads, Nob Hill was where the fruits were glossy, clean, and stacked like ancient pyramids, and cereal came in a box, not in a bag. Groceries were packed in paper bags, with someone ushering you to your car, if requested – así al estilo ricachon. Nob Hill was so American, I could see it but it felt out of reach, like most things.

I didn't know how much I disliked Eva until I stopped having her in my class. Her presence reminded me of everything I didn't have and everything I yearned for as a nine-year-old. She was pretty, pero con un splash de maldad.

Her true maldad wasn't revealed until we saw each other at church. Eva and her family went to San Patricio and for some reason we went to that church this Sunday. She took one look at Mamá, and locked eyes with me and gave me a pity smirk. Ya sabía mi secreto, so many questions must have been answered for her at that moment. I stood next to Mamá feeling ashamed for everything I couldn't be for her. Sentía el piso moverse debajo de mí y unas ganas de correr. How could she pray during el Evangelio and look at my Mom that way? I could hear Eva's voice interrogating me, despellejandome.

1. Why doesn't your Mom come to field trips?
2. Why do you always walk to school, even on rainy days?
3. Why doesn't your Mom come to Open House?
4. Why this?
5. Why that?!
6. And now, why does your Mom have a walker?

She knew now, and it was only a matter of time before the rest of the class would know.

Speaking only English made fourth grade challenging, I always felt stuck in translation. Living between two worlds and feeling like a stranger in both. My English was like broken concrete, walkable but not practical.

Nevertheless, storytime was my favorite part of the class. On Fridays, after reading a book we would "interview" a student, this time it was my turn, I was ecstatic about it until it dawned on me; Eva knows. Peers began to ask questions, and I answered. She looked at me with her condescending niña caprichosa smile. She raised her hand, with venom at the tip of her tongue, and snapped.

"Why can't your Mom walk?! Like, what is wrong with her?"

I caved into myself, como un caracol me escondí al sentir peligro, I instantly felt tan pequeña. She said it so matter-of-factly, so cold, so heartless. I blocked the sound around me, I could only hear mi corazón desesperado. Out of pride I kept my tears in and my mouth shut. I wasn't going to let her win, no le iba dar ese placer.

My teacher excused us early for recess, and during recess she moved my desk away from Eva. Aun así, ella continuó siendo E-vah. Y yo, el pajarito sin alas pero con unas ganas de volar muy, pero muy lejos: lejos de alli, lejos de ella, lejos de mi misma.

## Arroz con leche

When in doubt Mami would make arroz con leche. That was the last dish Mamá made before she resigned from the kitchen. En voz alta nunca lo dijo but she was heartbroken when she couldn't cook anymore. "Ya ni puedo cocinarles arroz con leche," decía con la mirada caída y con un tono depresivo. This was the dish Mamá was famous for, the dish requested for holidays, the dish that made a rainy day a good day. There was nothing more pleasant than to arrive home from school to the delightful smell of canela y leche hirviendo. The smell was simplistic and always consistent; the way it smelled is exactly the way it tasted. Un postre que Mamá nos hacía, y siempre le quedaba a la perfección. A Mamá le sobraba el ingrediente más importante: la paciencia. "Tienes que darle vuelta y vuelta para que no se humedezca la leche y para que el arroz no se recueza." El arroz blanco tiene que ser de la marca Jasmine porque el otro arroz no se cuece bien. La azúcar blanca tiene el sazón de Mamá, y la canela de la Esperanza Market porque es de Mexico y pinta la leche de un color morado, y claro la leche. Mamá parada sostenida por el rin de la estufa, Mamá con su bastón, Mamá con su walker y una silla por si se cansaba, Mamá sentada en su silla de ruedas alargando su pescuezo como tortuga para ver la leche hirviendo y solo cuando era necesario se levantaba lentamente con la ayuda de su walker. Mamá y su arroz con leche; a mi nunca me ha quedado como le quedaba a ella. Me hace falta su paciencia.

## Es una puta

Ale and I eagerly waited to hear the beep, beep, of Papi's troquita, so we could run outside to meet him. If we wait for another set of beeps, he would say, "Usa la cabeza, usa la cabeza mamacita," frantically pointing to his forehead.

This particular morning I was feeling pretty good, and we made it to his troca by the second beep.

It is an early summer day and we are half asleep, lagañas still peeling from our eyelids like mosquitos secos. But nothing matters, we get to spend the day en Corralitos with Papi. I love the drive to Corralitos; todos esos redwood trees abrazándome through the slim roads make me feel like I am inside of a lullaby y no puedo dejar de sonreír.

Papi's troquita siempre será uno de mis lugares favoritos. There is something comforting about the smell of dry dirt, cigarro y sudor.

We made our way out of Main Street, away from our overcrowded apartment complex, to Green Valley passing the hill that goes to Rolling Hills, y nos vamos hacia Freedom Blvd donde estaba la K(ay)Mart and finally to the calm roads of Corralitos.

Corralitos: the outskirts of Watsonville where some of the sweetest apples are grown. Donde por la mañana se puede ver el sol estirándose, dejándose ver solo entre las ramas de los árboles, besando la tierra tiernamente cada amanecer.

Papi would come in waves, in and out of my life, y yo ilusionada lo esperaba solo para verlo ir de nuevo. It had only been a few years since Papi had moved out, and started a new family. In those few years, I had already learned not to expect much from him. Siempre solo lo mínimo, pero al mismo tiempo toda una vida en esos momentos compartidos.

En su ausencia aprendí que cada minuto se saborea, porque tal vez ese pedacito de vida no se volverá a dar.

We would drive to three different ranchos to make sure the trabajadores had what they needed for the day. I would roll down the window on those rides to hear the platica y canciones de los campesinos. Some would work under the sun listening to the wholesome voice of Juan Gabriel while others indulged in a cumbia sabrosa como, "Que lindo tu cucu" y otros pasaban el tiempo reminiscing about their native lands. Todos en su ritmo, todos en sus mundos, creating a mundo of their own aquí.

Papi was creating yet another mundo within his world. Y en este mundo, my sisters, yo y Mamá salíamos sobrando. During this time Papi was renting a house between two apple orchards, the one that had a pond with little ranitas, rana eggs and giant sperms swimming in círculos como locos buscando salida. I liked this pond. A veces yo también me la paso dando vueltas sin poder ver más que ese instante. Watching the frogs jump gave me hope.

On our drive to his home we stopped by la marqueta del Chino, he told us to grab three snacks each. We got chips, water and unas paletas. Mine era de coco y Ale's de limón. Finally we drove down the road to his home, he often insisted we go inside and have lunch, I always said no. Going in would be a gesture of accepting the situation and I was far from that.

Besides, at that time I was still very much convinced que ella nos quería hacer daño. So when I was with Papi or near his home, I was never hungry. Dad went inside, Ale and I stayed with the ranas, la tierra y nuestras paletas.

There was a large black water tank towering over us, echándonos un ojo. I'm not sure whose idea it was, but instead of eating my paleta, I used it to write what was on my mind. My little sister, standing feet away from me didn't say a word, but I knew she had my back. She just watched my masterpiece unfold as she licked her paleta. I became *Harold and the Purple Crayon*, only that my crayon was a coco-flavored Michoacana paleta. I only had one chance to get each letter right. The day was hot and my crayon was melting at a fast rate, I could feel the milk and coco flakes dripping through my fingers. At last, it was done.

IVON ES UNA PUTA.

I wrote, and the heat waves gave my art piece an extra pop that I wasn't expecting but delighted it turned out that way. I took a couple of steps back and joined Ale who was licking the last bit of her paleta and moving on to her chips. It looked GREAT! All in CAPS, the period at the end made it a statement. I mouthed in a whisper, lo dije en un susurro:

IVON ES UNA PUTA.

Before I could celebrate myself, pasó un trabajador de mi Papá. Le llamaban el Payasito porque en México así se ganaba la vida. Y al llegar a los Estados Unidos también intentó su carrera de payaso, pero no tuvo suficiente fama. Al Payasito no le pareció gracioso mi propaganda y corrió a decirle a mi Papá. Mi Papá salió, ya algo molesto. Papá no es de carácter fuerte, pero venía hacia nosotras acomodándose sus pantalones y enderezando su postura.

"¿Tú escribiste esto?" me preguntó, con un cigarro listo para encender.

"Sí", le contesté. Ya estaba preparada para la cachetada.

Papi lit a cigarette and stared at the water tank for what seemed a lifetime. Luego he walked back and forth, from the water tank to the sperm pond, until he finished two cigarettes. He grabbed the water hose and pointed to the water tank for a few minutes.

Nada.

He did it again.

Nada.

El sol and the water tank stood in solidarity. Después de tres intentos se dio por vencido.

"Usa la cabeza. ¡Usa la cabeza mamacita!" He took a brief pause to build courage, "¡¿Por que Cristal, por que?!" Papá grita.

"¡Porque es cierto!"

Papi lit yet another cigarette. We got inside his troquita dejando atrás Corralitos hacia Freedom, y de Freedom regresando a mi mundo. Only this time, I had stopped swimming in circles, and I jumped. Ese verano I wrote :

## Cosecha

When I was young, my Dad would take us to the apple orchards. Sometimes, I would sit in the back of his pick-up, my feet dangling awaking the loose dirt. I would stare out into the orchards attempting to count the trees. I would never get past three. I would lose myself in the moment, as if I were traveling through time looking for my Dad, always reaching towards the idea of him.

Y allí lo encuentro siempre, en las huertas de Watsonville. Y caminó hacia él.

Caminó, una pierna tras otra. Con cada paso mis pies se enlodan un poco más. Cada paso pesa más que el último. Son las seis de la mañana y el cuerpo resiente el frío del campo. Llevo tiempo caminando con mis piernas enlodadas, pero es ahora, en medio de la brisa, oliendo la riqueza de la tierra mojada, caminando hacía mi padre viejo, que pienso en todo el lodo que yo he cargado por tantos años.

Y cuánto dolor me ha causado. Camino buscando a mi Padre, pero también a mí misma. La niña que aún se encuentra por estas huertas corriendo al lado de su Papi. I wave to him from afar, y comienzo a llorar.

I begin to feel angry – for the years that have passed, for my silence, for not knowing how to forgive him, for the love I still have for him.

Mientras que mi Padre se acerca, I have the urge to tell him everything.

Me hicieron daño Papi y tú no estabas,
Me hiciste falta
y no te encontrabas en casa.

Me hicieron daño Papi
y tú no estabas.

Con mis piernas exhaustas y mi pecho frío, I say nothing. Mejor camino a su lado, intentando conocer de su vida en el campo, su vida sin nosotros, his life.

Somewhere between the loose dirt, the blistering heat, the singing and joking of compañeros, between the orchards to the paved streets of his home... I don't recognize my father. And he doesn't recognize his daughter.

The roots stand but our branches have grown apart.

## Ruega por nosotros

Ruega por nosotros, ruega por nosotros, ruega por nosotros. En el nombre del Padre, del Hijo y del Espíritu Santo, Amén. I went to bed too often to the sound of my mother praying for us. Rogando por respuestas, begging for my dad to return in the middle of the night. Rogando por mejores momentos para ella, para nosotros. Mamá didn't know that, just a wall away, I too begged. I prayed for Mama's heartache to find relief, I prayed for courage, I prayed to be set free from my thirteen-year-old culpa.

En el nombre del Padre, del Hijo y del Espíritu Santo, Amén. Íbamos a misa cada Santo Domingo, nuestra iglesia era La Asunción en Pájaro, la iglesia de los campesinos; pequeña, humilde, pero llena de comunidad y caras familiares. Durante los tiempos de lluvia, a veces se inundaba La Asunción e íbamos a la Iglesia San Patricio. I didn't like that church, everyone stared at my

Mom as if she were some kind of vanishing miracle. Their eyes slowly followed her as she dragged her walker through the marble floor. They stared at us as we struggled to sit and stand Mamá up after each lectura. This church was the cathedral of our little town, made of brick, gold, e hipocresía.

For some reason here, I felt further away from God.

At La Asuncion at least we had a few things in common: todos hablábamos español, the majority of us knew enough about each other, so there was no need to explain the obvious, y nadie tenía un carro del año. Even knowing all that we knew about each other en esta parroquia, there was still so much unspoken. Tanto silencio atrapado, seeping through the layers of turtlenecks and sweaters and the gold Virgencita medallas. I could see it, feel it. Las madrecitas holding on to dear life to the banquitos as they kneeled during communion, eyes bursting with lágrimas as the song "entre tus manos . . . está mi vida señor . . ." would play. Los hombres siempre serios y cansados, and I felt it even more when we asked for forgiveness.

"Por mi   culpa, por mi gran culpa…" we all would say in unison; suffocating on what we couldn't bring ourselves to say out loud. The secrets that burned somewhere between the chest and throat, the secrets that die before they reached the tongue. El veneno that keeps us coming to church begging, rogando for a better version of ourselves, porque en los ojos de Dios, we are not enough. Y yo at a young age understood the señoras that cried as soon as they walked into la iglesia, here we were regañadas, humilladas y calladas.

Over time my prayers evolved:

I prayed for strength in my legs as I walked to Rolling Hills. I worried about the chaparro stranger that followed me every morning to school in his white van.

Yo le rogaba a mi cuerpo que dejara de brotar. I wanted to keep my breasts from blooming. But instead I found myself praying for numbness.

I prayed to be invisible. I wanted my uncle to stop looking for me.

Yo rogaba que el tiempo se regresara, que mi padre viera el daño que su ausencia me haría. I prayed, yo rogué y recé para que el tiempo me regresara la niñez que siempre soñé.

Pero Dios no escuchó, how could He? La iglesia had silenced my voice and baptized me con vergüenza.

I couldn't understand how God could be a silent spectator. For many years I lifted my heavy right fist and pounded my chest . . .

Por mi culpa . . . por mi culpa . . . por mi gran culpa . . .

Por tu culpa Dad, tantos me lastimaron,
breaking me in pedacitos.

Por tu culpa Dios, mi Madre nunca volvió
a caminar, bailar, ni amar.

Por tu culpa, culpo a mi culpa.

Ya no es mi culpa, it never was.

I release my fist, allowing the venom to run through me, and leave me. Then I go back for the little thirteen-year-old me, kneeling in front of a cross, I get her up . . . she's finally free.

Libre.

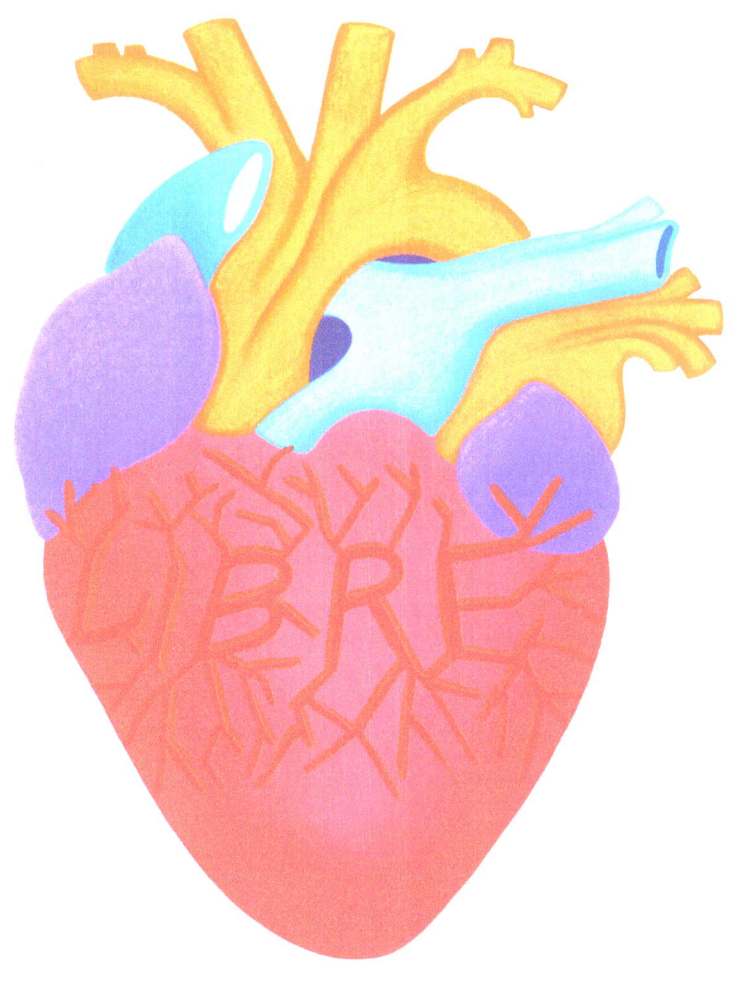

## Feliz

I'm happiest when Mom smiles, when out of the blue she lets out an exaggerated laugh, over some joke only she knows. Some joke stored in her past, somewhere in her little pueblo, cuando era niña, y se ríe– laughing and laughing until she runs out of breath. "Mami, ¿de qué se ríe?," I ask. She attempts to retell the memory but gets lost in laughter once again. That's when I'm happiest–when Mamá comes back to us. When I see her eyes light up with a mixture of inocencia y travesura, cuando su sonrisa ilumina la habitación.

Cuando su corazón le recuerda todos esos momentos que la hicieron feliz.

VIOLETA

## Se llamaba Violeta . . .

DAD: Mija, ¿te gustan las mujeres?

ME: Dad! No, why? Jeez.

DAD: Porque, no boi-friends for chu, ¿no hay
pretendientes por allí?

ME: I just don't want to date.

DAD: Es lo que pensaba, eres muy mujercita
para ser marimacha.

I met her during my senior year, waiting tables
at a local breakfast place in Watsonville.

ME: Two orders of chicken strips.

VIOLETA: Con o sin fries?

ME: Con.

VIOLETA: You got it .

ME: You cut your hair. It looks good.

VIOLETA: You noticed. Hey, you trying to hang out? Like
going out for coffee or something?

ME: Yeah sure, cool. Get my number.

Violeta scrambles to get a napkin and pen. She scribbles my number down and puts the napkin in her pocket.

VIOLETA: I'm gonna call you.
ME: Okay, and I'm going to pick up.

Less than a week later we went out for a cup of coffee near the Santa Cruz Boardwalk.

ME: I don't come to Santa Cruz often.
VIOLETA: It's pretty here.

And we just sat there and stared at each other and back down at our coffee. Until I couldn't take the silence anymore.

ME: So this is what hanging out is all about? Drinking organic coffee and staring at each other?
VIOLETA: I mean, we can talk too.

In this moment I come to realize that we are both very much alone, isolated from our families, swimming in a pool of questions, paralyzed by our past, betrayed by more than one. In these two hours, we find comfort in each other's stories. En este momento, we are no longer alone.

She leans in for a kiss. My body is overwhelmed by her closeness. I'm heated instantly, my nipples stimulated, my lips shivering, and I have the urge to go pipi. I open my eyes, and there she is.

VIOLETA: Is it okay?

I smile, so she leans in again. She kisses me and I don't stop her. I am in awe. Her lips are tender and fragile. It's as if I'm kissing myself and I feel myself fighting my arousal. She kisses my lips tan suavecitos como si estuvieran hechos de azúcar. Oh she kisses, she kisses aquí y luego acá.

Y de repente la voz de mi Papá, "Eres muy mujercita para ser marimacha," ringing in my ears.

ME: We should go, it's getting late.

I drive her home. We don't say much; el silencio lo dice todo. What now? ¿Confesión con el padre regañón? Ten to fifteen Ave Marías can't save my soul! Shit! I kissed a girl. Oh my God! My dad is going to kill me!

VIOLETA: ¿Qué haces?

ME: Praying... I mean thinking.

VIOLETA: You're thinking of praying?

ME: I don't know, maybe.

VIOLETA: Did it feel good? Did you like it?

I can't bring myself to say it, so I just nod yes.

VIOLETA: Entonces, you don't have to ask for forgiveness. Pray instead that this happens again.

I stop the car. She gets off. I avoid making eye contact; I'm not ready to see her.

VIOLETA: So what, you like me, huh?

ME: Ah . . . No. I don't think so.

VIOLETA: Yeah, right. You're thinking about the kiss right now, ¿Verdad?

I nod yes.

VIOLETA: I knew it, me too.
ME: Yeah okay. See you at work.

She walks to her door, y yo me voy. I didn't think I liked her, but her lips tasted like cantaloupe, and she was just like me. She too was seeking love. She understood what was happening at home–I didn't have to pretend, no tenía que dar explicaciones, not with Violeta. She was the eldest of four, her Pops left a few years ago, she dropped out of high school to help her  mom with the bills. She was only a year older than me, but her two jobs a day to help provide for her family had riped her at a faster rate.

When we spoke about struggle, we understood each other's wars. She kissed me. No one had ever kissed me with such tenderness. Sus intenciones eran puras, en sus labios no había mentiras. Con ella, mi cuerpo no tenía miedo. Esta sensación era nueva para mí; with each kiss she liberated me of any shame. With each kiss, she was restoring an innocence that was taken from me. We saw each other six times outside of work, and every time, I swore it would be the last.

I wait for her outside, I honk, she walks out fixing her hoodie. She gets in, leans in for a kiss.

VIOLETA: I missed your lips.
ME: Why do you say things like that?
VIOLETA: Because it's true.

I reject her kiss this time, and I look away.

ME: I can't. I can't do this to you. And whatever you're feeling towards me, don't. I like it but I can't like you like that.
VIOLETA: ¡Chale! Just like that?
ME: Yeah, just like that. I'm sorry.
VIOLETA: That's too bad, because I like you, and would have treated you right. I would have touched you right, made love to you right.
ME: Violeta, I don't want to hurt you.
VIOLETA: Don't worry about me. Just say it, you're scared.

ME: Yeah. I'm scared. I don't know myself like you do! I'm scared of this. Someone hurt me, and all of this still feels it. I'm sorry, I don't know what else to say. VIOLETA: You don't have to. I get it.

She opens the car door, she leaves.

Maybe, I could have continued with it all, and played the game even if I didn't know the rules. But, in the end I would have left. I would have used her, because selfishly, at that moment I needed affection. Y todas esas cositas que el cuerpo desea, por el simple hecho de ser cuerpo, pero no por amor. Pero ¿para qué mentirle?

Violeta was sweet, muy dulce, with a hard shell, y tenía un lunar oscuro en su mejilla que me enloquecía.

## PEDACITOS

I am made of pedacitos - little pieces. The pieces of me that were never enough because she was never enough. ¿Por qué creí esas mentiras?

¿Cómo fue que dejé que todos los demás me convencieran que ella no era suficiente? She is the biggest part of me, and it's taken me so long to see it. She was never broken, not like everyone else. She is made of some other kind of skin. Ella es puro corazón.

That's what keeps her light on: que en todos ve algo hermoso. Her ability to find joy in all the little moments in life, es como mirar las estrellas por la primera vez. Con el rosario entre sus manos y su inmensa fe, siempre encontrando una salida, una razón para seguir. Through the hardships, her head held high, she fights, and we fight alongside her.

Seven year old me,

"Mamá quiero ser actriz."

The sound of the cascading rosary beads
between her fingers fills the silence.

"Si eso te hace feliz, hazlo."

The only pedacito she ever needed.

## Con amor y agradecimiento:

Alfredo, Vida Mia y Luz Divina

Mis hermanas: Diana, Vane, Taly and Ale

Maestro Luis Valdez and Lupe Valdez

Rosanna Alvarez

Jose Cruz Gonzalez

Phil Esparza

Maribel Martinez

Ricardo Vasquez (Presente)

My students

Nuestros queridos campesinos

El Teatro Campesino

San Benito Arts Council Individual Grants

# Acknowledgments

**Elizabeth Cisneros** (Editor) is a Spanish Lecturer at UC Merced, with an interest in Mexican literature and culture. She earned a Bachelor's degree in Spanish from UC Davis and a Master's degree from Sacramento State. Born in Sonora, Mexico, she immigrated to California as a teenager, becoming a first-generation college graduate. Cisneros is passionate about language learning and cultural awareness, inspiring her students to pursue their dreams through education. She has presented at conferences on language and identity and contributes to projects promoting biculturalism and bilingualism.

**Ariel Mar** (Illustrator) is an Artist from Salinas, CA. Ariel received her education in Illustration and Design at the Art Center College of Design in Pasadena, CA. She draws, designs and prints all of her own work and is inspired by the landscape and culture of the Salinas Valley. Currently Ariel teaches and enjoys working with students and their families to create beautiful works of art from the heart of Salinas.

# Author's Note

When my sister Vanessa turned fifteen, I wrote in her Quinceañera recuerdo book... "Life is pesada." Yo tenía diez años and a chueco mushroom haircut. We laugh about it now, but maybe life did seem like a heavy load of laundry at that age. My person wasn't big enough to unpack y entender todo lo que estaba pasando. Entonces me aferré a mi imaginación y soñé beyond my limitations as a means to survive algunos momentos. Pero el cuerpo y el corazón todo lo siente y resiente. Ya no quiero correr de estos momentos, mejor me siento. I sit next to little Cristal and I honor her journey with these stories.

These memories son mías, pero tal vez también son tuyas. And if these memorias are familiar to you too, holdyour little person close to your heart and fight (lucha) for them.

Apapachos,
Cristal González Ávila

# About the Author

**Cristal González Ávila** is the daughter of campesinos. Born and raised in the migrant farmworker town of Watsonville.

She grew up a first generation Chicana, surrounded by fields of fresas y huertas de manzanas, emblematic of the agricultural work that shaped her family's livelihood. Her storytelling practice is deeply rooted in honoring her antepasados, in knowing de dónde viene y hacia dónde va—connecting her Mexican roots to the central coast of California.

With over fifteen years of experience, she has served the Central Coast as a multidisciplinary artist, bringing the stories of her community to spaces, stages, and film. As a playwright, her works shed light on critical social issues. *La Sombra (The Shadow)* is a one-woman show that explores domestic violence and the recurring, cross-cultural cycle that keeps it in the shadows. *La Cortina de la Lechuga* is a call-to-action play that highlights the housing crisis in East Salinas and other rural campesino towns. *Piernas: The Story Between Our Legs* is a powerful narrative of resilience and struggle, reflecting the challenges faced by families everywhere.

She is passionate about the transformative power of theater, the necessity of artistic expression for all children, and the profound impact that art can have on individuals and entire communities.

Learn more at www.cristalgonzalezavila.com.